SCOTTISH SAIL
A Forgotten Era

Charlestown, Fife 1880's

By the same author
Over Snape Bridge (East Anglian Magazine 1967)
Woodbridge and Beyond (East Anglian Magazine 1972)
East Coast Sail (David & Charles 1972)

SCOTTISH SAIL

A Forgotten Era

Robert Simper

David & Charles

Newton Abbot London
North Pomfret (VT) Vancouver

0 7153 6703 X

LOC Number 74—81055

TO PEARL

Set in 11 on 13 pt Baskerville
and printed in Great Britain by
REDWOOD BURN LIMITED
Trowbridge & Esher
for David & Charles (Holdings) Limited
South Devon House Newton Abbot Devon

Published in the United States of America
by David & Charles Inc North Pomfret
Vermont 05053 USA

Published in Canada by Douglas David &
Charles Limited 3645 McKechnie Drive
West Vancouver BC

Contents

Introduction

Some sailing ships have become legendary, their names and exploits have been handed down in numerous written accounts so that they will never be forgotten. The clippers of Aberdeen, the square riggers of Leith and Dundee and the huge steel barques of the Clyde already belong to the literary folklore of the sea. A great deal of information on these deep-water ships has survived and so too have a handful of the actual vessels either as restored museum ships or as hulks rusting away in whatever quiet backwater fate left them. Some of these square riggers are included in this pictorial record to remind us what they looked like in the far-off days when they were new and the latest thing in maritime transport. There has always been a romance connected with sailing ships, men became very attached to them, probably because being propelled by the ever-changing elements the ships seemed to be alive and have a kind of animal soul. But for all this the later square riggers were the products of an already industrialised society. For instance the Clyde shipyards, although unsophisticated by modern standards were in the 1880s turning out sailing ships at a rate which might well be envied by their later counterparts.

The main theme of this book is the sailing vessels in the coasting trades. At the beginning of this century there were hundreds of them working round the coast, but now virtually no trace of them remains. All that we have to remind us of this era that was so quickly swept away by progress are the details in official records, old photographs and the memories of the few surviving seamen. By combining these, something of this forgotten age can be reconstructed. To have delayed it a few more years would have meant that much of the personal side would have been lost. Indeed since few people connected with small cargo ships had neither time nor the inclination to keep written records much has already gone, but the gap in time is not yet so great that it is beyond recall.

The development and decline of the sailing coaster is closely linked with the smaller ports. Both evolved slowly but surely, from the end of the Napoleonic Wars until the close of the golden Victorian age only then to discover that the twentieth century had no use for either of them. Because of the difficulties of making a passage under sail Scotland discarded sail earlier than most parts of Europe. There were of course other coast lines which were just as hazardous, but Scotland was deeply involved in world trade and being at the centre of a huge global empire had financial returns flowing into the country. Although no-one would suggest that the nineteenth-century profits from shipbuilding and trade were spread over the entire population it did make capital available for progress. Victorians saw honest commerce as the only sure way to overcome the problems of what was then real poverty.

This meant that when a large company of ladies and gentlemen attended a

Traders at Stranraer

reception in the drawing loft of Black & Noble following the launching of the schooner *Mary Stewart* in 1876 at Montrose and drank a toast to the 'prosperity of the vessel', they were thinking of the benefits her construction had brought to the whole community. The same is true of a glowing report in the *Daily Free Press* following the launching at Aberdeen of the iron barque *Quathlamba* in 1879. This was the twenty-third sailing vessel, and incidently the last, before they went into steam, owned by Rennie's Aberdeen Line of Clippers trading to South Africa. The paper was largely acclaiming the city's commercial achievements. Some thirty years previously the Banff Town Council had made a report which showed that not only were the town's traders employing some 137 men but the ships' owners were actually receiving upwards of 30 per cent return on their capital. Naturally this was in the far-off days when sail was unchallenged at sea, but it shows how shipping brought rewards which a community, however hard they had worked in joint effort, could not have achieved without commerce.

The movements of the Banffshire sailing vessels showed that the merchants in the mid-nineteenth century were playing the markets and sending their freights wherever they could get the best returns. Most of their grain, herrings, salmon, cured pork and live cattle went south to London. Capital was employed also into ventures in whaling and sealing in the frozen north and in sending immigration ships to Canada. In the 1850s when Banff had reached its peak as a sailing ship port nine barques were owned here and some of these were in the Australian trade. About this time there were once twenty-six schooners counted lying in the harbour. There was a regular trade in oatmeal to the Highland ports and the barques sometimes loaded oatmeal as an outward cargo to Australia.

Although these ships were in international trade the commercial eyes of Banff remained firmly focused south. In the opening decades of the nineteenth century there had been passenger smacks sailing regularly to Leith and London. The London traders averaged nine voyages a year although the *Sovereign*, in her first year, made sixteen voyages to the Thames.

It was the cattle trade schooner *Boyn*, however, which set up a record that everyone talked about for years when she went to London and back in only eight days. Of course she was lucky in having a fair wind both ways. 'Driving' live cattle south was once a steady work for Moray Firth traders. Later a steamer called regularly each week and at Cullen live cattle were ferried out to her in small sailing boats.

One feature in which sailing traders differed from the steamers which took their place was that the sailers usually retained the same name throughout their career, no matter how many times they changed owners or port of registration. They were quite happy to use the same name over and over again. An owner ordering a new craft often gave it the same name as one he had just sold and the two vessels then continued trading from the same port. Everyone connected with local shipping knew clearly which ship was which, but it led to obvious confusion with the clerks who attempted to keep the records straight at some distant customs house.

There was for instance a schooner called *Mary Ann* trading from the Moray Firth. This was a very common name, but although everyone locally knew she belonged to Captain John Simpson of Portgordon there were around a hundred other similar coastal traders with the same name. Finally in 1906 a 'one name, one ship' regulation came in as section 50 of the Merchant Shipping Act.

Herrings in barrels were regularly exported up to World War I. There was a short burst of glory in this trade during the Franco–Prussian War of 1870 when good money was made by running the blockade into German ports. Ships used to wait at Elsinore and when there were no warships about and a fair wind blowing for the German ports, they snatched a quick passage.

One ship, the *Guiding Star* of Buckie made three such voyages in a year and virtually paid for herself. The next thirty years until the end of the century saw sailing vessels steadily improving and these were the great and glorious decades in which the sailing ship men fought hard to prove they could beat the steam kettles. By 1900 it was no longer really a commercial proposition to build new ships and a kind of countdown for the extinction of those still trading had begun. Scotland had played a leading part in the history of sail, but since it was virtually the birth-place of the steam ship, sail vanished very quickly from the northern ports.

Trading smack and convertie in the Clyde off Gourock

The term coaster really belongs to the steamship era, the sailing vessels we are dealing with were usually known as traders by the men who sailed them. They went wherever cargoes could be profitably transported.

In the late nineteenth century the Baltic and Newfoundland ports were still being visited by the larger traders. The *Leormundo* of Inverness was actually lost on one of these ocean voyages when she ran on King's Sons Rocks west of Labrador in 1897. The Wick schooner *Bonnie Lass* loaded salted cod at Scalloway in the Shetlands in 1893 for a Spanish port and a decade later was still making voyages to the Baltic with herrings in barrels. For these voyages outside British home waters a certificated master was engaged, the coastal skipper often signed on as a supercargo. Later a vessel over 100 registered tonnage was supposed to have two certificated men aboard for a foreign voyage. It did of course put costs up, therefore, human nature being what it is, there were a great many schooners built on the basis of being no more than 99 registered tonnage. But this was only delaying the inevitable for the steamships first drove them from the ocean trades back to the coast and here road transport and motor ships finally finished them off.

The Moray Firth traders often loaded oats for Aberdeen and returned with granite chips for roadmaking. Another regular trade was loading potatoes in bulk or wood, pit props or sleepers and then sail south to Sunderland and return with coal. Where there was no harbour they ran up on a beach. Often part of the coal was discharged at Cromarty or Invergordon and then the schooner, drawing less water, would be able to get to the scattered farming communities further up the Firth.

A couple of miles west of Invergordon is the old stone jetty called Belleport Pier. Now abandoned, it was once a busy spot. The local shipowner, Mr Hall

9

actually built a small schooner *Sisters* here but his best schooner was the *Halls* which was eventually lost in Tees Bay. A little further north at Tain on the Dornoch Firth there was only a beach but traders discharged here and in the Victorian period the *St Duthns*, *Gem* and *John* are remembered as being owned here while the *Tay* traded right up to Bonar Bridge.

The fishing industry of the east coast of Scotland provided a few freights. The Shetland schooner *Columbine* and the ketch *Bertie* used to go south to load barrel staves for the herring industry. Timber from the Baltic was once such a regular run that Captain Henry Smith's Portsoy schooner *Lily* and the *Craigowan* had square ports cut in their bows through which timber could be loaded. This practice seems to have been discontinued by 1900. With old battered ships a timber freight sometimes kept them afloat even though the hull was full of water. Such was the case of the barque *Professor Johnson* which in about 1910 was towed into Lerwick after being dismasted in a gale. It was later found that part of the lower hull had literally fallen out, but her firewood freight kept the barque afloat and indeed she was actually towed to the mainland in this state.

There were a few cargoes out of the normal run. The Ayr trading smack *Crusader* usually worked grain and coal freights to Ireland as well as in her home waters, but she also did quite a lot of work carrying gunpowder. The Orkney ketch *Thomas Henry* did two 70 ton peat freights from Eday to Fort William and well into the 1930s the Orkney traders were taking kelp (seaweed) to the Firth of Forth. It is a great temptation when writing any history to refer to a situation as being typical of a certain period. Indeed you have to, but it is worth remembering that all these ships and the trades they were in were slightly different. What was the proper way to carry out some operation on one ship may have been absolutely forbidden on another. The seaman's way of putting it was 'different ships, different long splices'.

The coal trade was by far the largest occupation of the sailing traders. Every town and village had a little group of vessels which brought coal from the most convenient area. This usually meant from Ayr on the west coast and from Bo'ness on the east, but by far the largest number sailed from the Rivers Tyne and Wear further to the south. Some of the distances these small craft sailed seems unbelievable in the light of modern forms of sea transport. The Shetland trading smack *Mersey* built as a Mersey pilot cutter in 1847 was still bringing coal to the islands from Sunderland when she was over seventy years old. On arriving off the River Wear she was taken in tow by a steam tug first to Carney's Wharf to discharge the gravel ballast and then to the South Dock to load coal. With 70 tons in the hold, the hatches were put on and then three tarpaulins, each coated with Stockholm tar, were neatly tucked in and tacked down before shipping the battens and wedging. After this the *Mersey* was towed to sea and if she was lucky would reach Shetland in four days, by which time this stout old smack and her crew of four had sailed over 800 miles just to collect 70 tons of coal.

Whenever two sailing vessels were sailing within sight of each other their crews were constantly watching to see which was the fastest. This keen rivalry afloat extended right down to the smallest craft. In the Firth of Clyde the Bute trading smacks were keen on racing, the first one into port ran up a red pennant displaying a crowing cock to the mast end. The last of these smacks to be built is reputed to have been the *Fairy Dell* built by Archibald Boyd at Ardrossan and launched in July 1897. She was ordered by Angus Kerr of Lochranza, Isle of Arran and he skippered her for many years in the coal trade across from the Ayrshire ports. About eight smacks were still working from Bute in the early 1920s, but by then, like the rest of their kind on the west coast, they were rapidly being put out of business by the steam puffers.

Everyone tried to avoid the Pentland Firth. With the tides racing between the Atlantic and the North Sea it could be a very bad place to be caught in adverse conditions in a small wind-driven craft. The Orkney traders could not avoid the Pentland Firth and over the years a high proportion of them were lost in it. In February 1900 the schooners *Pulteney* and *Maggie* were bound north in company. The weather was obviously breaking up and the master of the Wick *Pulteney* followed the usual custom of sailors in these northern waters and ran back to shelter in the Moray Firth. The *Maggie* stood on towards Stromness and that was the last time that anyone saw her. Much the same thing happened to the little 46 ton ketch *Elizabeth Jane* which was on passage from Leith to Wick with oilcake. She was last seen near the Pentland Skerries and no trace of the ketch or the two Orkney men on board was ever found.

Another probable victim of the Pentland Firth was the Thurso schooner *Isabella*. She was last seen leaving Sinclair Bay, Wick in November 1918 while on passage from Sunderland to Stromness. And so it went on year after year with monotonous regularity. The schooner *Mary Grace*, a Solway trader built at Irvine in 1871 was making only her third voyage under Orkney ownership when she was lost on Swona in June 1927. She had actually got some fifteen miles south of Clythness when a gale sprang up and she started to run back for shelter in Longhope with four reefs down in the mainsail. Later fog came down and she ran on the rocks near the spot where the *Annie Marie* had been lost only two years before.

Some of these vessels went on trading to an incredible old age. The Shetland schooner *Columbine* was eighty years old when she was finally broken up in 1914. Only slightly younger was another Shetland schooner the *Ariel* when she was sunk by German shell-fire in World War I, for she had been built in 1844, ten years after the *Columbine*. The point with a wooden hulled vessel was that they could periodically be rebuilt so long as they remained a commercial proposition. The amount of original fabric that remained after all these years is debatable, in some wooden vessels very little remained and the name was the oldest part of them. However, Lloyds ruled that when these rebuildings took place, however extensive, they could not be classified as new ships.

Most of the schooners were expendable. Built with limited capital that was available in a small seaport they had to pay for themselves in a few years. Many were very stoutly constructed however, and gave about fifty years of hard service, but this was almost an accident. When they were launched the men who had scraped together cash to purchase shares or in the case of the sailmakers and ships chandlers had given the ship credit, all were hoping for a return in the not-too-distant future. Sailing ships are surely one of the most attractive forms of transport ever devised and certainly I find every aspect of them intriguing, but when the return on capital began to dwindle, as it did in the 1890s, no more ships were ordered.

A trader, through careful handling by her skipper, could be made to last longer than her contemporaries. In the case of the *Columbine* her longevity was certainly not due to being in a sheltered trade. She was running coal from the mainland and returning with barrels of herring and occasionally going to Norway for logs. But the crew of five of this elderly trader were fond of her and nursed her when occasions demanded. One fine May morning in 1912 when she was on passage with coal from Burntisland to Lerwick the trawler *Prince Consort* emerged from the mist and hit the schooner's bows. The jiboom bowsprit was knocked into the water and the bows were smashed in. While preparations were being made to tow the *Columbine* to Aberdeen the young cook and seaman, J. G. Copland noticed the figurehead 'our Good Lady' floating in the water and went to some trouble to rescue it. He thought too much of the old schooner to let her crowning glory be lost.

This type of incident was too common to attract much publicity, but once the small Shetland ketch *Columbine* was part of what became a national story. Before the construction of roads on Shetland, everyone journeyed either on foot or by boat. A Sumburgh woman called Betty Muoat wanted to take her hosiery to Lerwick to sell it and boarded the ketch at Grutness. When the vessel was some distance from land the wind increased and the skipper was knocked overboard. The man and boy who made up the rest of the crew jumped into the boat and rowed off in a vain attempt to save their skipper.

While the man and boy were searching, the sails on the ketch filled with wind and she headed out to sea with only Betty Muoat on board. Realising it would be fatal to follow the ketch the two in the boat had no choice but to make for the shore. On reaching land they rose the alarm and all available craft, including the local mail steamer *Earl of Zetland* went out to search. However, there was no sign of the *Columbine* and she was given up as lost.

Ten days later word was received from Norway that a vessel had been seen drifting and when boarded a semi-conscious woman was found. The vessel was manned and taken to harbour. Betty Muoat was landed safely and looked after until she was able to travel and then she was sent by passenger boat to Newcastle and from there to London to be a guest of Queen Victoria. From London she was sent to Edinburgh where a great reception was waiting for her. The

12

Skiff *Dawn* 69 RO at Kilchattan Bay, Isle of Bute, June 1923

saga of Betty Muoat ended when she returned to her native Shetland. She spent the rest of her life in her native parish where she died in 1918.

Scottish Sail is told as a photographic history because we live in an age when people are accustomed to having information presented to them in a pictorial form. When Basil Lubbock published his books on sailing ships in the inter-war years photographs were used merely to back up the words. Illustrations were of course then very expensive, but Lubbock was writing for a public who had either seen sail in its prime or could go down to the nearest port and see the remnants of it. When Basil Greenhill's superb *Merchant Schooners* first appeared in the early 1950s they had to have good photographic coverage because by then fewer people had actually seen a true working ship. The maritime books by E. J. March really are the first to use photographs to bring back the past. This 'seeing is believing' trend was further advanced by Basil Greenhill and Michael Bouquet. Perhaps television has made us less inclined to believe written accounts, let alone find time to actually read them. Anyway, thanks to many photographers (usually now untraceable by name), we can see a little of what coastal sail was really like. Of course in such a short record the full history of every port and ship cannot be covered. I hope you will bear with me for picking on a few places and ships to illustrate what was typical of their era.

The view above of sailing ships at Aberdeen shows the wooden three masted barque *City of Aberdeen*, 586 tons gross in the centre. This barque was built by the well-known Aberdeen builder Duthie in 1862 and her name was dropped from the registers thirty years later. Ahead of the *City of Aberdeen* is the brig *Princess Royal*, probably the brig of that name which was built at Swansea in 1851. These were typical wooden square rigged ships which were built before the introduction of mild steel in about 1884 which allowed very much larger vessels to be constructed.

Many of the Clyde-built four masted barques were constructed so well that they far outlasted their original purpose. One of these was the *Olivebank* seen below which was built by Mackie & Thomson at Glasgow in 1892 for the Bank Line. In 1911 she was scuttled while on fire at Santa Rosalia but was raised only to sink again at the same place four months later. After several changes of ownership the *Olivebank* was acquired by the famous sailing ship owner Gustav Erikson in 1925. With six other Scottish-built barques she went on voyaging between Europe and Australia until World War II. These ships could only get cargoes by offering the lowest possible rates and this meant that they received the bare minimum of maintenance, yet they were still in the ocean trades when over forty years old. Tragically the *Olivebank* was lost on 8 September 1939 off Jutland after hitting a mine. Most of her Finnish crew who were returning after a voyage round the world went down with her.

The *Moshulu*, built by William Hamilton of Port Glasgow in 1904 survived competition from steamers which sent most of her contemporaries to the breaker's yard. She survived years in the Australian grain trade and was sunk in a Norwegian port during World War II. After being floated again she then had a succession of owners and was towed from one European port to the next, never having a real purpose or proper maintenance, but no-one quite liked to finally destroy this reminder of the wonderful age of sail. After four years of lying neglected in a corner of Amsterdam the *Moshulu* was towed across the Atlantic in the autumn of 1972 in twenty days to New York, where she arrived rusty but still afloat seventy-two years after she first took to the waters of the Clyde.

One of the most active builders were Russell & Company who had three yards on the Clyde. Above is the full rigged ship *Cambuskenneth* built by them in 1893. The *Cambuskenneth* has the Blue Peter flying at the foremast showing that she is about to leave the snow covered hills of her native Scotland to begin a career as an ocean wanderer.

The *Cambuskenneth* was one of the many ships which was sold to Norwegian owners when Britain had finished with sail. Her end was dramatic, for in June 1915 when ending a long voyage from the west coast of America to Queenstown with 3,000 tons of wheat she was sunk by gunfire from a German submarine. The first mate and seven of the crew were German and the submarine picked these up while the rest of the crew carried on in the lifeboat to Galley Head.

The Clyde's connection with deep-sea sailing vessels more or less died out in the first decade of this century. The last of the four masted barques to be built on the Clyde was the *Archibald Russell*, 2,354 tons gross. She was built by Scott at Greenock and was launched in 1905 for J. Hardie & Company of Glasgow. The ship was built as a memorial to Archibald Russell who had been a personal friend of Captain John Hardie and they had met almost daily to talk about shipping affairs, particularly sailing ships which they had both been keenly interested in. The *Archibald Russell* was originally in the coal trade and was sold to Gustaf Erikson of Mariehamn in 1925. She survived the World War II only to be broken up in 1949.

The last square riggers built on British yards for British owners were the three masted barques *Sunlight* and *Rendova* built in 1906 by Napier & Miller at Old Kilpatrick, Glasgow. They were sailing tankers which could load 2,200 tons and were intended to bring coconut oil in bulk from Rendova Island in the Pacific to Lever Brothers soap works at Port Sunlight. Both these barques were sunk by submarines in World War I, the *Sunlight* in 1915 and the *Rendova* in 1917.

Above is the four masted Russell-built barque *Mozambique* being towed from the Clyde at the start of her maiden voyage On the right is the Norwegian-owned barque *Alida*, 414 tons gross seen at Russell's Kingston yard in 1893. Note the more or less complete lack of machinery.

In the later years of deep-water sailing ships, Glasgow was the home port of the famous Bank Line. The company actually took this name when it was formed in 1905, but for two decades previously a fleet, most of them having names ending with the word Bank, was well known in the ocean trades of the world. It was all started and directed through tricky waters of maritime commerce by one man, Andrew Weir.

This was the age of tremendous expansion in world trade and steamships were already a common sight at sea. Weir and many other similar shipowners no longer attempted to build clipper ships which could out-sail the steamers but concentrated on sailing vessels which carried large cargoes cheaply. A year after buying the *Willowbank* Weir bought the small barque *Anne Main*, and then his first new ship, the 1,492 ton barque *Thornliebank*, was delivered by Russell & Company, Port Glasgow. By then Weir had sufficiently proved himself as a shipmanager to attract capital to keep on building and buying more ships. The exact number of ships being owned or even managed by the company is now difficult to determine, but until the Bank Line finally went over to steamships forty-four sailing ships were owned or managed by Andrew Weir & Company. Most of these were four masted barques built on the Clyde. Typical of these is the *Levernbank*, built by Russells at their Kingston yard in 1893 and seen here anchored in the Clyde before her maiden voyage.

The *Levernbank* was called a 'bare-headed' barque because she only crossed five yards on each square rigged mast, unlike the clippers which had a further sail, the royal above these. Here she looks very smart with painted gunports like the old men-of-war. Later like her sister the *Laurelbank* she was painted grey and arrived back from her ocean wandering with rust-streaked top sides. The *Laurelbank* only lasted five years because she went missing after sailing from Shanghai to Portland, Ore in 1898. The *Levernbanks* career lasted sixteen years for she foundered 300 miles west of the Isles of Scilly on 20 September 1909 while bound from Bilbao to Cardiff.

Russell & Company were among the most successful shipbuilders in the sailing ship boom of the last two decades of the nineteenth century. From their yards at Cartsdyke, Greenock and Kingston and Bay yards Port Glasgow came a continual stream of fine steel square riggers such as the *Cambuskenneth, Alida* and *Levernbank*. That these ships were beautiful is unquestionable but they had a depressingly high accident rate.

Such was the case with the *Ben-Y-Gloe* which never even carried a cargo to its destination. She was full rigged ship of 1,719 tons gross built by Russell & Company at Port Glasgow in 1886 for Watson Brothers, Glasgow. This brand new ship was towed from the Clyde south to Penarth where she loaded coal for Singapore. The *Ben-Y-Gloe* was towed from here at the beginning of October and got as far as Lundy Island when in very bad weather the towrope broke and the captain decided to run back for shelter under Nash Point. Here she anchored but the gale caused both cables to part and the ship was driven ashore on the rocks.

All the crew went up into the mizzen rigging except the carpenter who went up the main mast. Later during the awful night this mast 'went by the board' and no trace of the carpenter was ever found. In the early hours of the morning the tide had gone down and as the seas were no longer breaking over the wreck the captain ordered them down into the saloon. The gale had prevented the people ashore from getting a line aboard, but now fishermen climbed over the rocks and came aft calling: 'Is there anyone alive?' An apprentice who had joined the ship for his first voyage said: 'When we came on deck they told us to go up to the village and they would look after our things, which they certainly did because we did not see them any more.'

Ashore they had a miserable time until the Earl of Dunraven sent for them to be taken to one of his estates near by. Three other ships had been lost in the same gale. Here we see all that remained of the *Ben-Y-Gloe*.

The schooner *Scotia* below is seen loading on Carsethorn beach in 1903. Now little remains of what was once quite a port at Carsethorn except a few old posts with rusty chains sticking up out of the shore. This is just one of literally hundreds of places round the Scottish coast to which small traders worked under extremely exacting conditions. The *Scotia* was one of a large number of vessels owned over the years by Captain Willy Robson of Carsethorn. Robson's last craft was the tiny pointed stern schooner *Petrel* which he bought from the Auchencairn coal and lime merchant Heugan. The *Petrel* only loaded 38 tons but made countless trips across the Solway with potatoes and back with coal, before she was broken up at Carsethorn in 1932.

After taking on a pilot off Carsethorn most of the traders bound into the River Nith followed the narrow channel to either Glencaple or right up the river to Kingholm Quay just below Dumfries. Most of the Solway traders were registered at Dumfries although few ever ventured that far up. The two berths in the little dock at Kingholm were kept clear by trapping the tide on the marsh area behind the river wall and then at low water by opening the sluice gates allowing the water to rush out and sweep the silt away. As in the neighbouring port of Annan Dumfries during the 1850–60s, barques and brigs engaged in the ocean trades. Nicholson actually built small clippers at Annan for the China trade while timber came annually to Dumfries from the St Lawrence River. The coastal trade was almost all directed south and Liverpool was the focal point of the Solway trade right up until it ended quite abruptly at the end of the 1920s.

Dalbeattie became a leading Solway shipping port in the 1890s because so many ships came there to load granite sets that they would offer low freight rates just to get a cargo north. There was also a brick and tile works there sending cargoes south, so that freights which might have gone through other ports came to Dalbeattie. In the narrow River Urr there were at least sixteen traders at the same time at Dalbeattie. Above, the topsail schooner *Bengullion* is in the process of being turned in the turning berth in 1906. Behind in the narrow harbour is the *Maggie Kelso* a well known Urr schooner commanded by Captain Robert Edgar. Behind her is the Kippford owned trading smack *Earl Grey* which worked mostly to the Solway beaches.

Just below the turning berth the warehouses still stand where J. Carsewell & Sons had their animal food delivered by their topsail schooner *Warsash* until she was burnt out during the disastrous fire at Kingston Dock, Glasgow in 1914. Carsewell later had the schooners *Solway Lass* and the *Bengullion* which were the last owned here. Eventually most of the Solway traders used to come to Kippford for repairs although William Cumming built some sailing vessels here. Notably the three masted topsail schooners *Try Again* and *Balcary Lass* in 1867 and 1874 respectively. Both were locally owned for their whole careers, the *Try Again* was run down and lost with all hands in the Bristol Channel in 1906 and the *Balcary Lass* went missing while carrying salt fish from Labrador to the United Kingdom.

The Solway shipbuilders gave their smaller coasters 'outdoor' rudders and most of them were launched with tiller-steering, variations of which, were used by builders from the Menai Straits up to the Clyde as on the *General Havelock* (page 23) which was built at Beaumaris. One of the fastest traders in the Liverpool Solway Trade was the two masted topsail schooner *Margaret Ann*; built at Barrow it had the Lancashire version which was a rudder outside a tiny counter stern. With virtually pointed sterns they were often condescendingly referred to as wherries.

Before the ever-moving channel of the River Nith reaches Glencaple a small creek called The Pow branches off on the west side and winds its way inland to near the village of New Abbey. At the head of the tidal Pow, Bog Quay was built in 1842. Due to the Solway's 30 ft tide range there was always enough water in the Pow and horses, one on each bank, had to tow the traders up the narrow but deep channel. Above, is the little topsail schooner *Sweetheart Abbey* which was built at Bog Quay but as this was not a suitable site she was the only one built here. Actually this view of her was taken when she was up on the slipway at Kippford for repairs, but the man in the centre of the group is her builder.

The other view on the right is the schooner *General Havelock* at Bog Quay in about 1930 which shows just what a rural spot it is. She was owned by the Kingans who used her in connection with their farms and timber business. Pit props were carted down from James Kingans saw-mill to Bog Quay and stacked up waiting for the *General Havelock* to arrive back from one of the southern ports. Usually she was away for about ten days and returned with animal food from Liverpool. This schooner only loaded 70 tons but sometimes other schooners were chartered like the Dumfries-owned *Ocean Gem* which could load about 120 tons. In about 1924 an engine was fitted in the *General Havelock* and skipper Willy Tate and his mate could handle her, but while under sail only a boy was necessary also. James Kingan of Lane Side told me how when he first took a lorry to Cumberland and back in a day the whole district was amazed. Not long afterwards the 'wee schooner' was sold to John Nelson, but is was impossible to make her pay. Finally she was sold at Annan in the 1930s for breaking up for firewood for £5.

Below is another typical Irish Sea sterned topsail schooner at Dock Foot, Dumfries on the River Nith just above Kingholm Quay. The topsail schooner *Enigma* was a Solway trader with a shadowy past. She had been a slaver and smuggler in the Indian Ocean before her guns were removed and she settled down to jogging about the Irish Sea. The *Enigma* eventually sank off the Isle of Heston taking her crew down with her.

The tiny *Sweetheart Abbey* was also lost at sea while on passage from Stranraer to Campbeltown.

The river side quay at Kirkcudbright had been improved since these two views were taken. The three masted topsail schooner below has her two unloading gaffs aloft; discharging in such a fast flowing tideway must have been hazardous. Above in a dock at Kirkcudbright are the two masted tiller-steered topsail schooners *Daisy* of Whitehaven owned by the Kirkcudbright grain merchants Williamson & Son, and behind her the brigantine *Utopia*. She could load about 200 tons and was the largest of a fleet of traders accumulated by Captain Alexander Stitt of Kirkcudbright.

Captain Stitt also bought a well-known Barrow-built schooner at Glasgow and renamed her *Margaret Ann* after his wife. Although sometimes commanded by his son Alex, in 1903 Captain Stitt took over for a trip to Dumfries and his wife went along. While the schooner was anchored off Glencaple Mrs Stitt died on board and Captain Stitt never went to sea again and in fact died himself not long afterwards. Most of his vessels were sold after this.

Above is the wreck of the three masted barque *Firth of Cromarty* ashore three-quarters of a mile south of the Corsewall Lighthouse on the Wigtown coast.

The *Firth of Cromarty* left Glasgow on 20 August 1898 bound for Sydney and Newcastle, New South Wales with 2,250 tons of cargo, mostly cases of whisky. The barque had been built of steel ten years previously by Russell & Company at Port Glasgow. On what was to be her last voyage she left Glasgow with James Nelson as her master and a crew of twenty-three. Normally the tug would have just taken her down the Clyde to the Tail of the Bank but as the wind was unfavourable the tug took her as far as the Ailsa Craig before casting off.

The barque began to be hit by heavy squalls and the master thought about running back for shelter behind Arran, but kept on and at 9 pm on 27 August the Corsewall Light was sighted. The master believed the barque to be about nine miles off the Light. Around 11.15 pm the wind began to blow with considerable force and changed direction from NNW to WSW. Realising that the ship was now close to a lee shore the crew were called to wear ship. As they got ready to put her on to a fresh tack suddenly, through the squall, rocks loomed up and with an abrupt thud the ship's port quarter struck them. Ten of the *Firth of Cromarty's* crew left in one of her lifeboats and rowed round into Loch Ryan and the rest were taken off by rocket-line from the shore.

The Board of Trade Inquiry ruled that the master was to blame for the loss of the vessel and the cargo, valued at £50,000 and suspended his master's ticket for six months. Meanwhile whisky came ashore along the coast and even twenty years later Stranraer fishermen hauled up bottles of the stuff which were still drinkable.

Above, a small topsail schooner and a trading smack are discharging on the beach at Drummore. Strictly speaking we have now moved out of the treacherous Solway Firth, but as in later chapters I have used one term to cover a wide area. Opposite, above, we have moved round to Stranraer. The harbour at Stranraer really dates from 1863 when the steamer link to Ireland was opened from here, replacing the old Portpatrick–Donaghadee route. The top view is of traders at the Old Pier in about 1900. Below, two topsail schooners are laid up with the sails off at Clayhole in 1900. Schooners, or 'coal boats' as west coast people called everything from a smack to a puffer, used to discharge on the Stranraer shore to save harbour dues. In a northerly gale the wind funnelled up the six miles of Loch Ryan making Stranraer an unpleasant berth for a wooden trader.

The best known of the later Stranraer traders was the *Alpha* (page 49). Captain James McCracken remembers that in 1929 when he was master of the schooner *Twin Sisters* of Stranraer he was towed out of Maryport with the *Alpha*. Both schooners were deeply loaded and when sailing hard in a strong ENE wind the *Twin Sisters* was doing seven and a half knots, but in three and a half hours the *Alpha* on the same course was out of sight. In the Clyde with a fresh beam wind the *Alpha* was seen passing steamers doing nine knots, but in those days when the sail-steam rivalry was still burning strongly she tactfully stayed out of spanner-throwing distance from their engine room doors.

26

Above is the *Severn* one of the rare auxiliary sailing ships to be built on the Clyde. The idea was to make the best of both worlds by installing a small steam engine which could be used in calms and save having to hire a tug for the long tows into port. The *Severn* was a true auxiliary in that she could obviously be handled properly as a sailing vessel. However, the auxiliaries were never widely adopted because the engine room and coal bunkers took up cargo space and they were twice as expensive to operate because both sails and steam propulsion had to be maintained.

The numbers of Clyde sailing ships began to accelerate in the 1870s and the custom of shipping companies giving their vessels names linked to a standard pattern began. At Glasgow there was Denniston's Island Line named after large world islands while Thomas Law's Shire Line had a patriotic flavour for their ships were named after Scottish counties. Also at Glasgow was the Bank Line while at Greenock there was the Shankland's Burn Line and Abraham Lyle's fleet of fine sailing vessels named after well known Capes. The Clyde yards were busy throughout the 1880s turning out new ships, in the opening years of the 1890s four masted barques were regularly leaving the yards, but this began to slow down and finally stopped altogether in the first decade of the nineteenth century.

The number of deep-sea sailing vessels flying the British flag declined rapidly so that by the time World War I started there were not many left. The Shire Line of Glasgow had kept some of theirs and even had the *Berwickshire* and *Kinross-shire* after the Armistice was signed. Finally even these went and sailing ships with the traditions and deep-rooted prejudices that went with them faded from the seas.

Above is Girvan on the Ayrshire coast in about 1900. The fishing skiffs on the right are probably Saltcoats boats which worked on the Ballantrae Bank and used Girvan to land their catch. These skiffs replaced the cutters (see bottom page 30) and were in their turn replaced by a later skiff (top page 32). There is a tendency to talk about 'traditional' boat types as if the old types were fixed, in fact each generation tended to evolve a slightly different version to suit the current trend.

On the south bank can be seen the Marquis of Ailsa's little steamer *Nimrod* which was built at Ailsa Shipbuilding Company's yard at Troon, a firm the marquis also owned. Behind the skiffs is the topsail schooner *Fairy Queen* owned by the Givran grain merchants Hutcheson & McCreath. On the north side of the harbour was a berth where coal was loaded from the collieries at Dailly, Kilkerran and others near Girvan. Most of the coal was shipped to Belfast sixty miles away.

One of the ships on this regular run was the *Innistrahull* which one night reached the harbour in a severe gale. She was hanging on to a mooring on the South Pier and was about mid-stream paying out to bring her up along side the coaling berth on the north side when out of the darkness came the *Fairy Queen* making a dash for the harbour before the gale. Unfortunately she did not know the *Innistrahull* was there and crashed through the mooring ropes. The *Innistrahull* was set free and drifted on to the north breakwater where her crew were able to get ashore but the vessel was a total loss.

On these two pages are the three main types of craft used in the inshore fishing around the Clyde estuary and locks. The two opposite came originally from lantern slides. Below is the *Jean* at Saltcoats in the 1890s, she was one of the transom sterned smacks which were about 30–2 ft long and were engaged in drifting and trammel-net fishing. Also sometimes line fishing and lobstering in the different seasons. However in the 1890s they were replaced by the double ended skiffs which were evolving out of small open rowing boats.

The view above shows the *Freeth* and another nabbie leaving Saltcoats. The nabbies were a version of the double ended skiffs. Above we see the perfected version of these in the Loch Fyne Skiffs at Tarbert in 1912. Like the nabbies these were single masted half decked luggers. The Loch Fyne skiffs were rather lightly constructed and seem to have not lasted very long. Their beautifully shaped hulls were kept light to make them fast, for fishing in an area where gales occurred frequently the fishermen wanted a craft that could reach shelter quickly.

On the west coast the fishermen went in for a standing lug sail and usually referred to their boats simply as skiffs, they were never called zulus. This term belonged solely to the east coast where they had huge dipping lug craft referred to as yawls and occasionally further defined into fifies and zulus.

The harbour at Saltcoat was constructed between 1684–1700 for the coal trade between Scotland and Ireland, but most of the trade had gone by 1835 when neighbouring Ardrossan expanded.

31

In the summer the herring arrived off the west coast and the boats followed them along the coast. Above, in the late 1880s, the herring fleet is leaving Stornoway on Lewis in the Outer Hebrides on a still evening. In the distance are some large yawls from the east coast while the gaff cutters in the centre are from the Clyde. In the centre are the trading smacks *Advance* and *Jessie* of Stornoway. The 30 ton *Jessie* was built at Fraserburgh in 1850 and the *Advance* was built at Kingston on Spey in 1884. These smacks, before steam came, served as passenger boats taking people south when they went to seek seasonal work in the Lowlands.

Above opposite is Tarbert in about 1903 with clinker-built Loch Fyne skiffs on their moorings. The next generation of skiffs on the Clyde were like the ones in Campbeltown, September 1922 seen below them. They are slightly bigger half decked skiffs and by this time all had engines and sail had become the auxiliary. Bowsprits had already been dropped by the Clyde fishing fleet because of the introduction of ring-net fishing. On the right the schooner *Moses Parry* of Dublin is waiting to load coal. The Clyde ring-net fishermen referred to themselves as trawlers to distinguish their method from their bitter rivals the drift-net fishermen. Herrings for the fresh market were actually bought at sea. The buyers followed the fleet in small steam herring 'screws', and when the skiffs had caught herring they lit a flare and the buyer steamed over to strike a bargain. The loaded screws then steamed flat out to the nearest railhead.

Because the pairs of ring-net skiffs had to make a close circle round a shoal of herring they drew 6 ft aft and only 2 ft forward making them very handy.

Above is the iron topsail schooner *Mary Stewart* with her sails drying seen sometime before 1902. This schooner survived until the end of the sailing ship era and there was often confusion with a wooden *Mary Stewart* which also outlasted her contemporaries. It is as well to describe the careers of both *Mary Stewarts* starting with the iron one seen above which was built by the then new firm of Black & Noble at Old Shore, Montrose in 1876. The schooner was launched by Miss Milne, daughter of Provost Milne and was ordered by Captain James Stewart of Strone, Argyll. Captain Stewart was her first command and registered at Greenock she traded between the United Kingdom and Newfoundland. It is amazing to look back and realise that this schooner which loaded only 110 tons was profitably employed in the ocean trades. In the 1890s *Mary Stewart* passed to owners in Orkney and traded with coal to St Margaret's Hope. As she was fairly flat bottomed she was suitable for sitting on the sandy beach while coal was discharged into horse and cart at low tide.

Probably when this view was taken she was skipper-owned by William Weaver and trading on the west coast. Captain Weaver's thirteen-year-old grandson, another William Weaver left school to go to join the schooner. Like many of the schooner-trained men he eventually commanded an ocean liner. In Captain Weaver's time she was still classed A1 at Lloyds and later when she was trading as a motor ketch in the Bristol Channel a general survey showed that her hull was still sound when seventy-eight years old. She finally finished trading in the mid-1950s and the last report I could get of her was that she was lying in a Spanish port as a yacht about six years later.

The other *Mary Stewart* was even smaller but was also rigged as a topsail schooner. She was built by Barclay at Ardrossan in 1868 and had a pointed stern with outdoor rudder. This pointed stern seems to have been popular around the Clyde, not only with the gabbarts but also with small traders. The *Mary Stewart's* last owner was Donald MacLean of Tiree. In the late 1930s she was laid up in a tiny harbour at Scarinish and gradually fell to pieces.

A well-known Clyde mariner was Captain John Marshall of Maidens who was master of the Marquis of Ailsa's yacht *Lady Evelyn* in the 1870s. However, he only went to sea after a rather bitter experience working in Glasgow. When he finished school in about 1844 his uncle, John White, sub-governor of the South Prison, Glasgow, offered him a job with good prospects in the prison as a turnkey. But the youthful lad from Ayrshire was only fed on prison fare of bread and water. After several months of this he met his uncle in the corridor and asked how long he was to be kept on prison fare. John White was not pleased with such an inquiry and snapped back: 'Do not dare speak to your uncle like that.' Marshall at once threw down the keys and marched out of the prison for ever. Marshall went to sea after this and before taking to yachting was master of the Ayr trading smack *Crusader*.

In about 1870 Walter Kerr, a fisherman of Millport on Great Cumbrae Island switched from fishing to trading. Over the next decade he got together enough capital to order a new smack especially built for trade. Named the *Jessie Kerr* she loaded about 30 tons and cost £250 complete with sails and gear. Her builder, Fife of Farlie obviously lost on her construction because he said to Kerr 'Walter, when you ordered this boat it would have paid me to have given you £10 and sent you away!' Fife's reputation as a good builder must have been based on his conscientious craftsmanship, for he chartered the *Jessie Kerr* for her first freight, 25 tons of lead, and told Kerr: 'If she makes even a cupful of water when loaded I'll take her back.' Because of the tremendous strain thrown on the hull while discharging on the beaches she certainly needed to be strongly built. Cargoes were landed at Dowancraig for Portrye and Balloch farms.

A few years later Kerr had another smack, the *Mary Kerr* built by Fife. Most of their trade was with coal to the small harbours and piers on the Firth of Clyde and back with 'Arran' sand, often to Glasgow. Occasionally they went over to Kilchattan Bay at the southern end of Bute and loaded tiles. After a few years the puffers were more numerous in the Clyde and usually they gave the smacks a tow to help them along a bit. Above we see the *Jessie Kerr* and the *Mary Kerr* at Millport.

At the time this stern shot of the *Jessie Kerr* was taken she was taking a small part in a general election campaign. She is seen sailing from Millport to Arran with Rosslyn Mitchell, later MP for Paisley on board. He had been campaigning in Millport and it seems had fallen victim of a mysterious political intrigue which caused him to miss the steamer so that he could not get to Brodick that day to meet the Arran electors. Finlay Kerr saved the day by sailing him there in the *Jessie Kerr*.

In 1912 the *Jessie Kerr* was lost inside Horse Isle while entering Ardrossan harbour. The *Mary Kerr* had been sold to Arran owners and Finlay Kerr went to the east coast to find a replacement. Here he bought the 56 ft fifie yawl *Sisters* for £30 and took her to the Ardmaleish yard Bute, and converted her to the cargo ketch *Betty Kerr*. She traded between Millport, Troon and Ardrossan until 1926 when he bought the puffer *Saxon*. She was traded by Walter Kerr, Finlay's successor until 1965, thus for nearly a century three generations of the same family took part in the changes in Clyde shipping. Sail with the smacks, auxiliary sail with the *Betty Kerr* and finally high-pressure steam with the *Saxon*. The view below shows the Manx schooner *Goldseeker* and the French-built, Irish-owned ketch *Marie Celine* in Queens Dock, Glasgow.

The skiff *Deer II* is seen above at Kilchattan Bay, Bute in June 1923. At the jetty is the converted fifie *Vineyard*, a Peterhead fishing boat which was one of a number sold to the west coast for cargo carrying after the disastrous fishing winter of 1921. The *Vineyard* is unusual in that she kept her original name. The last of the sail-using vessels on the west coast was the *Halcyon* seen below at Campbeltown with her skipper-owner Captain William MacMillan standing left of the mast. He spent a lifetime in these waters and sailed with his father on *Village Girl*, *Duchess*, *Vineyard* and then bought the puffer *Norman* in 1930 and finally *Halcyon* in 1945.

Gabbarts and Trading Smacks

From the Mull of Kintyre right up the west coast to Cape Wrath there were numerous scattered towns, villages and crofts whose only trade link with the rest of the world was by sea. The Highland coast with its hills shrouded in mist and rain and grey islands rising out of the turbulent Atlantic is romantically beautiful, but as far as transport was concerned it was one vast geographical problem. On this gale-swept coast the small sailing craft dodged from one sheltered spot to the next making even a small cargo costly in time. The western islands had to wait for the steamships to bring them into regular contact with the industrial towns and the few simple goods which helped to make life less gruelling. Around the Firth of Clyde there was quite a large population scattered around ten locks and four large islands. These and the busy ports on the Ayrshire coast all looked to boats as a main means of transport. In the Clyde the sailing packet used to wait off Greenock pier for passengers to Dunoon, Rothesay and Lochgoilhead. Greenock was also the point of departure for the passenger smacks that sailed weekly across the North Channel to Belfast.

Above are representatives of two different types of west coast traders lying in the mouth of a burn under Brodick Castle, Arran. On the left is a gabbart with a fixed bowsprit and on the right a trading smack.

The Clyde, like most large estuaries had its own type of local craft which developed through regional maritime traditions to suit the waters they traded in. Known as gabbarts the prime aim was to be able to pass through the Forth and Clyde Canal locks and for this they could not be more than 70 ft long with a 20 ft beam and a draught of about 6 ft. The gabbarts had double ended hulls and were full bodied but never flat bottomed and could load about 70 tons. They had one large hatch with narrow side decks, no bulwarks although they had a rail round the stern. The outdoor rudder was controlled by a tiller. The rig was equally unsophisticated, just a single mast which could be lowered for canal work. The only sails were a large gaff mainsail and a staysail. Above is the gabbart *Mary* anchored off Hunter's Quay in about 1883.

Most gabbarts were built at Bowling and Dumbarton but very few were built after 1850. The type had died out by the end of the century but the name was far from dead around the Clyde and any craft with a faint resemblance to them was dubbed a gabbart or to use the Clydesiders pronunciation 'gaabart'. Craft like the *Lady Margaret* (see page 47), *Bee* and the Gigha Island-owned *Margaret Wotherspoon* are often still referred to by the longshore men who knew them as gabbarts, but they were really a later breed. Many of these, like the *Margaret Dewar*, 38 tons net, built at Ardrossan in 1874 started off as gaff cutters but were later converted to ketches. Lighters in the Forth and Clyde Canal were also referred to as gabbarts.

In a way the trading smack is the forgotten craft of the sailing ship era. The deep-water clippers, merchant schooners and most of the numerous local types have been duly written up but the smacks have been overlooked because they did not make record-breaking passages nor were they particular to any one locality. The Clyde with its waterside towns and villages needed small freights moved only a few miles and the tubby little smacks were well suited for this task. They remained a common sight here long after they had vanished from other areas, for even the railway could not rob them of their freights to the islands, particularly Arran.

Above is the *Glen Sannox* owned by Kelso of Corrie on the Isle of Arran not far from Glen Sannox. Built at Ardrossan in 1878 she was 40 ft long, had a 14 ft 9 in beam and when loaded drew 6 ft 3 in. It would be wrong to assume that the trading smacks were easy to sail, crews had to work just as hard as those on the big schooners. In the smacks on the following pages there are to be seen several blocks in the rigging on every halliard. By having a wip, ie block and tackle on the halliards, the crew could get enough purchase to get the sails up tight. The gaff mainsail called for the full strength of two men to control it, especially when running in a fresh breeze.

Above (opposite) is the *Glen Sannox* again, entering the tiny channel at Black-waterfoot on the west coast of Arran in 1911. The jib is kept set to balance the mainsail and also to leave the foredeck clear for working. The topsail has been stowed on the mast end of the boom. Astern are two open clinker boats, always called punts on the Clyde, showing that a local man had joined the smack to help her two-man crew with the task of getting into the narrow channel under the shadow of the hills.

The smacks provided a cheap form of transport but they were not very reliable or fast. The industrial revolution solved this problem with the steam puffer whose hull design was influenced by both the gabbarts and smacks. Because of their strong identity the puffers endeared themselves to the people of the west coast in a way the sailing traders never quite managed to. Sail is usually only remembered by those connected with it while the puffer has become the symbol of the west coast.

Below (opposite) is the *Betsey Crawford* at Carradale, an Argyll fishing village on Kintyre overlooking Kilbrannan Sound. She is in fact an Arran smack owned by the Crawfords of Corrie and had been sailed about forty miles across from Ayrshire with coal (the journey round by land would have been nearly a hundred miles).

A section of the rail has been lifted out so that coal can be discharged and the smack's punt can be seen behind the children. These heavily constructed boats were an important part of every smack. The punts did not have a mid-ships thwart and by not having a seat in the middle this space could be used to hold about three-quarters of a ton of coal. Often a punt load would be delivered at a loch-side croft. After the punt was loaded it was sculled towards the shore. Here a horse and cart came into the water until the horse was standing up to its belly. The boat came along side the waiting cart and the coal was shovelled in.

By the early 1920s when it was very obvious that sail was going to die out on the west coast, there were still about twenty sailing vessels owned on Arran and eight on Bute. Most of these were smacks loading 35–40 tons and some were converted Manx fishing dandies of the same tonnage. John Hogarth started sailing with his father at this time on *Minx* which was one of these. They were faster than the smacks but having a long fine-lined hull could not discharge on the beaches. The Butemen called the 80 ton smacks gabbarts if they had been built to go through the locks of the Forth and Clyde canal. These craft had little sheer in the hull and no overhang at either end. They set a good spread of canvas which included a jackyard topsail and a character-istic point was that when the bobstay was set up tight the end of the bowsprit tilted down slightly. Loaded, they drew about 8 ft and often traded right round Scotland. The last one remembered with the true cutter rig was the *Bee*. The others were converted to ketches because their mainsails were so difficult to control.

The trading smack belonged to the age of horse and sail. Top opposite is the 45 ft smack *Duchess* waiting to discharge at Kildonan on the southern end of Arran. Owned by the Cook brothers of Southend, Arran the *Duchess* had been built at Port Bannatyne, Bute in 1878. Below is the smack *Betsey Crawford* at Blackwaterfoot, Arran in 1934. Above is the *Hunter* discharging coal in 1908 at Kildonan at the same place as the *Duchess* opposite. By the mid 1890s the puffers had replaced the smacks on most of the west coast, but sail was still competing in the Clyde. The last two built were the *Betsey Crawford*, opposite, and the *Fairy Dell* in 1897. All these smacks had deep rather bulky hulls, the later ones had rather fuller sections than the earlier smacks but all were immensely strong which enabled them to take the ground loaded.

The *Fairy Dell* was built for Captain Angus Kerr of Lochranza and was skipper-owned by him until he was lost overboard. It is not known what happened but they were sailing in a gale and the mate came on deck to find he had vanished. After this it was believed that the ghost of Captain Kerr followed the ship and it is said to have appeared in times of stress to come to the ship's assistance. The smack was fitted with an engine in 1931. Four years later the motorised *Betsey Crawford* and *Fairy Dell* were still working out of Arran. The *Princess Mayse*, a Plymouth barge also with a motor, owned by John Hamilton of Irvine was working around Clyde until she was sold to North Devon in 1949. The *Fairy Dell* was converted to a Clyde fishing craft in 1947 and was used in the Clyde area when owned by Stanley Lipscombe. In 1955 she was sold to a Belfast man.

On the opposite page is the 23 gross ton smack *Elizabeth* laid up at Lochranza in 1936 after her trading career had ended. She was later sold as a yacht and even became a fishing boat in World War II. Actually she had been built by Boyd at Ardrossan in 1885 and was last owned on Arran by Donald Kerr of Catacol. Her straight bow and long keel must have given her quite a strong weather helm. This was used to an advantage because when they wanted to go about, the helm was put amidships so that the weather helm took effect and started to bring the bows up into the wind.

Above is the 40 ton register ketch *Lady Margaret* which represents a larger type of West Highland trader. She was built by William Fife & Son at Fairlie in 1876. Fife was mainly concerned with building yachts in the days when the rich really were rich. He always kept a trading smack under construction to keep his skilled staff together in the slack periods. He only built one other trader after this and she was rather unimaginatively called *Ketch*. However, Fife's traders were regarded as the best on the west coast for speed and construction. In 1937 the *Lady Margaret* belonged to John MacCorquodale of the Isle of Lismore.

MacLea of Rothesay, Bute built small smacks and schooners all with pointed sterns until his yard was swept away to make room for the promenade in about 1880. One MacLea schooner the *Elizabeth Ellen Fisher*, was later owned in Southern Ireland and not broken up until World War II.

Sailing coasters lingered on up to the end of the 1930s on the west coast while round on the east coast they were mostly sold to Irish and Bristol Channel owners shortly after World War I. A typical west coast man was Captain MacFadyen of Lismore Island. He was a Cape Horner and had a master's ticket but returned to the coast and bought the old cargo smack *Isabella MacMillan*. In 1919 he went round to the east coast and bought a 65 ton dwt Fraserburgh-built fishing boat. This he named *Mary & Effie* after his eldest and youngest daughters and fitted her out as a cargo ketch. Captain MacFadyen's twenty-two-year-old son John went as mate, having been with his father since he left school.

The *Mary & Effie* traded as far north as Orkney and south to Ireland, but most of her work was done in the Western Isles and mainland lochs. She occasionally delighted the MacFadyens by sailing at ten knots. In 1928 a Kelvin engine was fitted and after this the ketch was kept mostly to the inner islands and lochs until finally the puffers took all the trade.

The Kelvin had previously been in the attractive topsail schooner *Texa* which had belonged to Captain MacDonald of the Isle of Islay. Later she had been sold to an Irvine broker who had altered her to a ketch and fitted the Kelvin. However the *Texa* was later wrecked on Irvine bar and the motor was sold to Captain MacFadyen for the *Mary & Effie* which had a motor winch fitted at the same time. In this view below from the northern end of Lismore with the Appin Hills in the background *Mary & Effie* is ahead of the Captain MacCorquodale of Lismore *Lady Margaret*. Because of the lack of wind, both ketches are being towed by the crew in their boats.

In the early 1930s Captain Duncan MacCorquodale purchased the 75 ft schooner *Alpha*. She was then laid up at Kilkeel, County Down where she had been built in 1879 as a single topsail schooner. Her hull was pitchpine planking on oak frames and the *Alpha's* very shapely hull made her noted fast sailer with a reputation for leaving steam coasters in her wake. She appears to have had a trouble-free career trading between Irish ports and the Mersey except for when she was stolen in 1882 and found two years later in the Bristol Channel.

Captain MacCorquodale registered *Alpha* at Stranraer and kept her in the Solway coal trade. In 1933 the square topsail was removed and a small Kelvin auxiliary fitted, a wheelhouse was also added on her square counter stern. She was now competing with the Clyde putters and this meant further increase in power was needed so that a 60 hp Kelvin was fitted in 1938 giving her a speed of seven knots in good weather. At the same time she was altered to a motor ketch at Tarbert, Loch Fyne. This new cut-down rig allowed *Alpha* to pass through the Crinan Canal as she was by then trading along the west coast with a crew of three. The *Alpha* often loaded and discharged two or three cargoes in a week and stood up to this hard grind for fourteen years without mishap. The MacCorquodales were a Lismore family and in the photograph above we see her discharging on the beach at Port Ramsay at the northern end of the island. To the right can just be seen the masts of John MacFadyen's *Mary & Effie*.

When nearly seventy years old the *Alpha* was sold to Oban owners and traded a few more years. But then she was too out of date to remain a commercial proposition. Her two hatches were small, one being only 3 ft 6 in by 5 ft. This made a smaller area for water to get in while being driven hard under sail but these hatches were no good for modern loading equipment.

The scale of fishing and numbers of men and women and boys employed in it is borne out in the illustration above which shows the herring boats at Wick during the 1875 season. Above opposite is a view of the trading smack *Dunvedin* and a ketch loaded with coal at Bettyhill Pier on the River Naver in north Sutherland. Out in the river in the background is a salmon fishing coble. In Scotland a coble was an open boat with high bows and with a shelf in the stern on which salmon nets could be laid while being paid out as the boat moved away from the shore. The 48 ft *Dunvedin* is a trading smack which was a fifie bought on the east coast for £25 by 'Black Jock' George MacDonald. He spent a further £50 converting her to gaff and then began trading. The *Dunvedin* sometimes traded to Ireland with slate.

In the view below the trading smack *Balone Castle* is lying in the Kyle of Tongue and is dwarfed by the Sutherland hills. At the seaward end of the Kyle of Tongue, in the village of Talmine, at least thirteen smacks were owned between 1891 and the 1930s when just the *Balone Castle* was left making the occasional freight. All these were converted fifies except the counter sterned trading smack *Mary* which came from Broadford, Skye and the *Harlequin* which was a former oyster dredger.

There was an incident with a Tongue smack involving the Gaelic 'second sight'. A woman noted for her predictions went out at about 10 o'clock one night to get peat and returned to say that she had just seen the whole of the Kyle of Tongue light up and was sure this foretold a tragedy. Barely half an hour later men came running and knocked at the door asking for lanterns to help them search for a man who had been knocked overboard by the boom of the smack *Band of Hope* as she was tacking across the Kyle of Tongue. As it proved later, the man had drowned at the same time as the woman had her hallucination of light on the water.

On the northern coastline of Caithness the six miles from Scrabster to Castlehill were dotted with quarries, and thousands of tons of dress stone for street paving was shipped away from the area to ports all over Britain. Above are some of the stone traders in the Thurso River. Opposite, top, are three brigantines and two topsail schooners lying in Scrabster Roads in 1860. Scrabster harbour was very much smaller then than it is now. In the foreground is the Holborn Head lighthouse and below there was a place known as The Chains. Here traders lay stern-on, their bows held out by their anchors and their sterns made fast to iron rings set in the cliff-face. Below this is the tiny harbour of Castlehill into which the schooners had to be warped. The flagstones weighed around 2 cwt and we see them here being moved on special handbarrows. In 1900 seventeen schooners and ketches owned in Thurso were all in the flagstone trade.

The last Thurso-owned trader was the three masted topsail schooner *Thursonian* which was a typical soft bowed Baltic trader and was originally the Danish *Hossana*. Under the Danish flag she had been trading to Newfoundland and Labrador. Once when running at ten knots under bare poles she was pooped and a man who had been working aft was washed overboard. In 1905 she lost two men in one day, both from the yards of the fore topmast in heavy weather. Her period of ownership by the Thurso Company seems to have been a short period after World War I. She was finally lost on the Norfolk coast in December 1928 (page 55).

Above, a lug sail boat is passing Thurso Castle in about 1900. Below are two zulus at Castle Bay, Outer Hebrides in June 1937. These boats were then owned by fishermen from Barra and Eriskay, but their design, with sterns coming up to a point, shows that they came originally from the Moray Firth. The wheels are the horizontal type working a rack and pinion steering gear. Forward of this is an 'iron man' hand hauling gear which was in use before steam capstans were evolved.

The view above is of Lybster, one of several small fishing harbours on the southern coast of Caithness. This is believed to have been taken in 1860 and when I first saw Lybster a century later the scene was identical except that there were no boats or barrels of herring. I think by then there were only four motor fishing boats working from Lybster and this whole industry had virtually vanished. The hills along the coast were dotted with crofts, many of which were empty as people had had to go away in search of work. Just inland from Lybster on Camster was a deserted village with a lonely graveyard walled in to keep out the sheep.

In the above view a schooner is being loaded with barrelled herring and a trading smack in the foreground is probably doing the same. The fishing vessels pulled up on the pier are half-deckers. Originally open boats were used but the half-deckers were introduced in the 1850s, and this development was continued until a decade later when most of the Caithness boats were decked in as the single masted luggers are in this view.

Below is the wreck of the Wick schooner *Thursonian*.

Here in Orkney can be seen Stromness harbour in about 1887 from Brass's Pier (now Sutherland's), the crane in the foreground was still there in 1972. W. D. Shearer was a well-known owner here and his vessels had painted ports. The schooner bows on is probably his *Minnie* built by Carnegie of Peterhead in 1878. The *Minnie's* normal trade was to sail south in ballast or occasionally with kelp and load coal in the Forth at either Carriden or Charlestown, but it is also recorded in her log book that she went to Sunderland, South Shields and Amble after coal. Once she brought cement, lime and bricks as well as coal from Sunderland to Stromness. The Shearers had contracts to deliver barrelled herring to Germany and there appears to have been an attempt in 1901 to open up a market in Russia. The *Minnie* went to St Petersburg (Leningrad) with 500 barrels of fish oil, fifty of which were stored on the deck. The round trip from Stromness and back to Newcastle with a freight took nearly six weeks after which she resumed her coal trade. When she was sold to Belfast owners in World War I the *Minnie* was the last of the Shearer schooners.

Before the introduction of steamships Orkney's only connection with the outside world was by sailing craft. The Kirkwall clippers sailed a regular service to Leith and the last of these was the topsail schooner *Pomona*. The last Orkney sailer was the ketch *Rosedale* of Kirkwall which was broken up in 1949.

There was a saying in Shetland that 'Amsterdam was built on the herring bones from the back of Bressay'. This is the island that gives some eastern shelter to Lerwick harbour and the saying comes from the fact that the Dutch once fished these waters extensively. Above is Lerwick in about 1902 with the Dutch fleet arriving at the start of the June herring season. There are at least sixty-nine Dutch drifters in sight and in the foreground are the masts of the Scottish yawls and steam drifters.

As Shetland had to import timber, usually only fishing craft were built although the schooner *Janit Hay* was built at Lerwick in the 1880s. Hay & Company were the chief owners having the ketch *Buttercup* on which the herring were cured. This meant that they did not have to return to port every day but came in at weekends and the barrels were loaded straight on to a carrier bound for the Baltic. Hay's also had the *Alarm*, *Seagull*, *Nelson* and *Ida* which like most Shetland boats usually fished on the Foula Bank and off the Orcadian coast. They also had the old schooner *Columbine* and the trading smack *Prince of Wales* which went to Sunderland for coal. Some of the Shetland boats went to the Faeroe Isles and there is the well known incident of the 'turn-turtle' smack *Petrel*, which while on passage from Faeroe rolled right over. Luckily the stone ballast burst out through the hatch and this released the weight allowing the smack to roll upright again and survive.

Over on the west side of the Zetland mainland Scalloway was a thriving fishing port. It was alive with activity when the smacks were home from Faeroe and Rockall and the schooners came from the Scottish mainland to load herring. Grimsby men also came here to tranship their salted catch. One of the features of Shetland was that they abandoned the lug sails so beloved by the Scottish east coast men, and had huge gaff mainsails instead. This seems to have taken place by 1903.

Above is the Shetland 'fourern' or four-oar boat *Stanley Henry*. This type of boat was originally used for day fishing, but later the narrow version was developed for day racing. Opposite is the Shetland herring boat *Swan*. She was built at Lerwick early this century by a group working under the foreman carpenter John Shewan. When this view was taken in 1936 she was one of only three sailing fishing boats left in Shetland. Later this beautiful craft was sold to be a yacht on the south coast of England.

It was the custom for whaling ships bound from London, Whitby, Hull, Dundee and Peterhead to the Greenland Straits to call at Lerwick and recruit extra men. This started in the mid-eighteenth century and was at its peak in the middle of the nineteenth century when as many as fifty Greenlanders lay at anchor off Lerwick. The whalers often went ashore on wild drinking sprees while the townsfolk stayed behind locked doors hoping the whalermen would not set the town on fire.

Whaling was a very hard life, but some Shetlanders went every year and many passed a quarter of a century without seeing the green spring corn in Shetland.

Above, barely moving in the still air is the topsail schooner *Welcome Home* when she was owned at Portmahomack at the entrance of the Dornoch Firth. Built at Stornoway in 1881 this elegant clipper bowed schooner is typical of the mid-Victorian coasters, although each had slightly different features. The *Welcome Home* has a loose footed foresail and mainsail.

The topsail schooner was the favourite rig of the British coastal sailors. The square sails on the foremast gave the schooner extra sail area where it really counted. These sails were the equivalent of the modern yachts spinnaker. Most of the old time masters preferred the schooner to the ketch because a two masted schooner could be handled in confined water with just the gaff foresail set. In heavy weather most schooners stowed the gaff foresail and kept only a reefed mainsail and forestaysail set. The advantage of having the largest sail at the after end of the vessel was that it helped to push the bows up into the wind.

The sailing traders seldom sailed a very precise course but made their passages according to the wind direction. The modern compass is divided into 360°, but the man at the wheel of a schooner could not steer to the nearest degree. Instead the circumference of their compass was divided into thirty-two points, each point consisting of $11\frac{1}{2}°$ of the modern compass.

The Moray Firth builders seem to have been progressive in outlook and were the only British ones to give their topsail schooners patent reefing square topsails which meant that these sails could be stowed from the deck. The *Ythan* and *Alice* were taken a stage further by having a standing foregaff with the sails brailed into the mast. The *Alice* of Banff is remembered with some affection because her master, the stout Captain Main, always wore a bowler hat.

Below are the topsail schooners *Industry*, bows pointing, and the *Ythan* drying sails at Invergordon in about 1912. The *Industry* had been built on the Beauly Firth, but was later sold to Ireland. Captain Alex Murray of Invergordon bought her there, crossed to Runcorn and loaded salt which he took to Buckie via the Caledonian Canal. He traded her until the middle of World War I, and then, like so many of the Moray schooners, she was sold south.

The fine Moray schooner *Dispatch* was also sold south, but her Avoch owners tried trading again when they bought a Danish schooner which had been seized for debt at Hartlepool and they renamed her *Craigowan*. She was fitted with a steam-drive capstan which made handling the cargo much easier than it had been with a hand dolly winch. The *Craigowan* was beating up the Firth closely reefed in a hard blow when both masts went over the side. Her hemp standing rigging was thought to be the cause. The schooner was damaged by the spars pounding against her to such an extent that she sank but her crew were saved by a trawler. This was the last schooner owned on the Moray Firth, but the same owners next bought the ketch *Young Fox* and Captain MacIntosh who had had *Craigowan* and *Ythan* took command. Only a year later the *Young Fox* was laying storm-bound in Fraserburgh with the schooner *Tay*. It was blowing hard from the NE but both vessels decided to chance it, the *Tay* reached Dornoch Firth, but the *Young Fox* never arrived at Portmahomack, the exact fate was never known. Sadly Captain MacIntosh's son, who had planned to emigrate, had only sailed on this trip as a replacement.

Because the Cromarty Firth could be entered at all states of the tide it was a favourite place for coastal sailers to seek shelter. Before World War I a spell of bad weather might have caused twenty or thirty traders to run in for shelter. Above the Royal Navy ships can be seen lying in the Firth outside Cromarty Harbour.

The ketch *Leader* was once drifting on the tide down the Firth one calm day when she got foul of the torpedo booms sticking out from a battleship at anchor in the Firth. Both her masts were snapped.

The glimpse of a topsail on the horizon off the Moray Firth sent the pilot cutters racing out to reach the vessel first and put their pilot aboard. The occasional Baltic timber barque heading for Inverness was a prize really worth competing for. In the summer of 1895 the pilots heard from a timber merchant that a barque had left Finland. A few days later the 20 ton cutter *Forward Ho* slipped her mooring in Kessock Roads and stole down the Firth hoping to sight the barque first, but the Beauly pilots in their sturdy 40 ton *Vanguard* later joined in the chase. For a week the two cutters manoeuvred about the Firth, once they went as far as Wick, but always hunting for the barque. In the end high winds forced the *Forward Ho* to take shelter east of the Sutors of Cromarty, and from the hills her disappointed crew finally saw the barque arrive and their rival cutter thrashing out to put their pilot aboard.

The Moray Firth pilots divided themselves into two classes. The Beaulies who took the ships through Beauly Firth and into the Caledonian Canal and the river pilots who took ships into the River Ness. Originally they raced each other to every ship in zulu-type skiffs propelled by four powerful oarsmen but competition became so keen that they acquired sailing cutters to go further out.

Above is the topsail schooner *Bonnie Lass* of Wick at Cromarty in 1899. Below, the same schooner is being towed into Portsmouth. The *Bonnie Lass* was owned by her master Captain John Machean of Cromarty. In about 1908 while on passage in the North Sea an Aberdeen trawler crashed into the schooner's bow and a man working on the jib boom stowing the flying jib fell on the trawler's deck. The two ships parted and four days later the rest of the crew of the badly leaking *Bonnie Lass* were saved. Both sections of the crew thought that the other was drowned until they met ashore.

In this view we see the ketch *Colonel Moir* loading oatmeal in the old harbour at Portsoy circa 1900. This Portsoy ketch was skipper owned by William 'Wildie' Wood and the mate was his son-in-law John Hay. These two made up the entire crew although occasionally they shipped a third hand. The *Colonel Moir* is loading oatmeal from the mills of Mr William Ewing, a cargo the ketch traded regularly with to the West Highlands. Other traders brought bones to Portsoy to be made into bonemeal fertilizer and schooners also loaded cured herring for the Baltic ports here.

Amongst the last Portsoy schooners was the *George L. Munro*, skipper-owned by James Wood, brother of 'Wildie' Wood, which finished trading in about 1914. There were about a dozen sail traders owned in the port in about 1900 which included the *Cairncrankie* skipper-owned by George Wright and eventually lost at sea. Others were the *Lily*, Captain Henry Smith, *Pioneer*, Captain John Smith and *Olive Branch*, Captain Henry Osborne. Another Moray Firth trader was the *Tempus Fugit* which was wrecked at the entrance to Portknockie Harbour.

With the departure of the small unsophisticated sailing coasters many villages stopped having direct shipments. Until the end of the nineteenth century traders discharged on the open north Moray Firth beaches at Shandwick, Balintore and Hilton, which are on the open Firth and completely exposed to the easterly winds. In 1897 a small harbour was completed at Balintore and then there was regular schooner traffic. On the south side of the Firth, Nairn was the home port of schooners while a surprising number were owned at Findhorn. Further along the small harbours of Hopeman, Cullen and Banff were busy, but most had trouble with silting.

Below is Buckie harbour with the ketch *Annie Stuart* lying astern of the 185 gross ton barquentine *Natalla*. The *Annie Stuart*, skippered by Captain Henry Osborne of Portsoy traded fairly regularly to the continental ports and returned to Buckie with salt in bulk. The *Natalla*, built at Troon in 1879 was the largest Moray Firth trading vessel in the final years of sail. She was regularly trading with coal from Sunderland to Buckie and was one of three vessels managed by the local coal-merchant George McWilliam. The other two were the schooners *Lady Cecilia Hay* and *Koenisberg* which were both jointly owned by Captain Robert Reid, the Buckie ships chandler and William Cumming. Both schooners were lost at sea.

After the Spey River, Banff was the most important shipbuilding centre on the Moray Firth. Two fast schooners called *Boyn* were built here. One was a cattle-trader which held the record to London and actually carried the mail. The later one was a 'ninety-niner' which set up a record for sailing from Banff to Sunderland, loading coal and returning in three and a half days. Quite often a trader could take weeks on the same route.

The Macduff schooner *Alice* was built at Banff in 1878. Five years later she was returning from the north of England deeply loaded with a freight of lime when a heavy sea off Rattray Head washed the mate and three seamen off the deck and they were drowned. The master, his son and an apprentice were below and missed this fate, but a year later the apprentice was on the main boom reefing the mainsail off Yarmouth when the boom accidently jerked and he fell off and was drowned.

The main shipbuilding centre on the Moray Firth was at Garmouth and Kingston which are near the mouth of the River Spey in Moray. There is now no trace of shipbuilding on the River Spey, but this was once the leading centre in northern Scotland. The parish of Speymouth is made up of the small town of Garmouth and the village of Kingston-on-Spey. However, the natural forests inland were the most important factor in the story. Timber was floated down often as far as fifty miles inland.

The best known of the Victorian builders were the Geddies and the Kinlocks who all appear to have been related. They thrived in an age when most of the world trade was moved from small ports or even open beaches by comparatively small ships. Not only did Strath Spey provide good timber but the countryside was not disturbed by internal strife or wars which periodically put their continental rivals out of business. These were the days when Britannia ruled the waves and any ship flying the red ensign received preferential treatment in most foreign ports. The Kinlocks celebrated this prosperity by naming one of their ships *Britannia*.

Opposite we see William Kinlock, the yard-manager, on the left and his brother Andrew, who supervised the ship construction, on the right. Both look every inch the successful Victorian businessman.

Above is the Speymouth barquentine *Leading Chief* which like most of the Spey ships was registered at Banff. Built by the Kinlocks at Kingston in 1876 she was 124 ft long, 26 ft in the beam, had a 14 ft draught and was 315 tons gross. She is typical of the deep-water ships built at Speymouth and was the last of Kinlock's bigger ships to remain afloat when she was owned in the Channel Islands in 1907.

In all the Kinlocks built over fifty ships and most of these were 99 ton schooners. The Kinlocks launched two vessels a year and in their best twelve months launched 1,400 tons of shipping. Many of these were built for local owners and engaged in world trades. The largest vessel built was the 800 ton barque *Lord Macduff*. Owned by Captain MacDonald of Garmouth and engaged in the China trade she was referred to as the *Mighty Macduff* in the Moray Firth.

Kinlocks began to keep the ships they built and called them the Chief Line, although they were more widely known in the shipping circles as the Lockie Chiefs. There was the barque *Ocean Chief*, the barquentines *Scottish Chief*, *Wandering Chief*, *Leading Chief*, *Indian Chief*, *Kaffir Chief*, *Afghan Chief* and finally the *Moray Chief* in 1888. These were kept in the Cape, and East and West India trades. In the early 1880s the fortunes of Speymouth began to change, steam was beginning to replace sail and the Clyde was taking the lead by building in steel. Worse still the forests inland were exhausted and timber was having to be brought from the Baltic and North America. Also the Spey changed its course leaving Garmouth inland and the water was not then deep enough for launching. No doubt the astute William Kinlock saw these changes coming as he shifted his interest to managing the Chief Line.

For over a century and a half ships went from the ports of eastern Scotland every summer into the Arctic to hunt for whale and seal. The whaling grounds became almost as important to European economy as the modern oil and gas fields.

Traditionally both English and Scottish ships recruited a large proportion of their crews in Shetland. Life on board was grim; voyages were long and scurvy was common. In 1837 the *Dee* returned to Aberdeen with only nine of her original crew of forty-six alive and the *Advice* returned to Dundee with only seven of her crew of forty-nine. Discipline was tough as most of the crew were a rough crowd. In 1829 when ninety-two British whalers were caught by pack-ice in Baffin Bay nineteen ships were smashed to splinters. The 1,000 men set free roamed the ice drinking and looting in the riot known as Baffin Fair.

Dundee became the main Scottish whaling centre and the first auxiliary was built here in 1854. Peterhead was another centre but this had not joined in the Greenland whaling until the brig *Robert* sailed in 1788. The port's fleet was at its largest in the late 1850s with thirty whalers. By this time the ships that were built for whaling were incredibly strong. The Scottish ships were wooden, mainly oak sheathed with greenheart with rock salt layers to cushion the crushing pressure of the ice.

One example was the Peterhead three masted auxiliary *Eclipse*, built by A. Hall & Company at Aberdeen in 1867 she carried eight whaleboats and had a crew of fifty-six. She was 149 ft long and 441 tons gross—the maximum size for a Peterhead whaler. Because the port was tidal and vessels were limited in draught often a whaler returning deeply laden had to wait a few days for a large enough tide to get her in up to her berth.

The Scottish whalers were quick to introduce steam auxiliary engines which allowed them to move through the ice more easily. But they remained sailing ships with special features like patent roller reefing single topsails which could be furled from the deck and running gear arranged to keep the main deck clear.

Pushing further into the Arctic to find enough 'fish' meant spending one winter in the Arctic, and Repulse Bay at the north of Canada's Hudson Bay became a favourite wintering spot for the east coast whalers. Leisure time was spent playing football and even staging plays. Most whaling books speak of maintaining 'cordial' relations with the Eskimos. However, some were written by the rather puritanical New England and Scottish whaling officers reluctant to enlarge on this aspect. In the whaling regions most Eskimos can count at least one whaler amongst their ancestors.

Above is the Peterhead whaling brig *Alert* in the ice. The men in the bows are standing on the raised fo'c'sle head which has no rail. This was normal practice prior to about 1890 and there was nothing to prevent a man working on this deck from being swept overboard when the brig plunged into a head sea. A whaleboat is in the davits aft; these Scottish boats had a small transom stern. When hunting whales the boats stayed near the ship and towed their catch back to the whaler for cutting up, unlike the Americans who established shore bases.

Above is Captain Alex Davidson at the wheel of the Peterhead whaler *Alert* with his crew in about 1885. In the latter years it was only Dundee's thriving jute industry and its need for whale oil that kept the Scots in the eastern Arctic. By then only the occasional whale was being taken and only by killing seals, walrus and also trading and even mining mica could the ships be filled. There was however, very little profit in it once the bowhead whales had almost been exterminated.

Above, the whaler *Balaena* is leaving
Dundee. In 1913 the *Balaena* and *Morning*
returned to Dundee without taking a
single whale. The next year the *Active*
returned without even seeing a whale.
Peterhead's last Greenland traders were
the *Albert*, seen right, the *Rosie* which was
sold south and the *Vera* which was lost
in the ice.

Opposite top is the herring fleet crammed into Fraserburgh in the 1890s. Below this is Portnockie in 1938 with the *Olive Branch*, built at Cockenzie, left and the *Lark*, built at Boddam, right. Above is Stonehaven in 1904 and below shows the *Girl Pat* and other former sailing boats at Pennan in 1952. This Aberdeenshire village was once a fishing boat and trading smack building centre.

The scene above of Montrose salmon fishermen, tells the whole story of what a laborious business catching fish was to men whose only resources were their own strength and ingenuity. On the opposite page the crew of seven are seen on the Montrose fifie *Pilgrim*, ME 607. The *Pilgrim*, like all the east coast boats has virtually no rail, making the working space entirely open. Lying at the men's feet are the heavy sweeps and there are thole pins in the low rail to take the oars. The tholes would have been removed when sailing, but were shipped so that the yawl could have been rowed into port or at least have her drift controlled.

Virtually everything on a sailing ship was geared to the strength of a man. Even the large square riggers in ocean trades which looked huge had every sail aboard controlled by manpower. They did carry steam donkey winches, but these took a long time to get working and as coal cost money there was a noticeable reluctance to use them. On the fishing boats they did have steam capstans because they could not get their nets in without them, but everything else was a dead pull. There was a lot of back-breaking heaving, but in many ways the sailing vessels never outgrew the men who sailed them.

Some small sailing inshore fishing boats were worked on the Moray Firth until World War II. They were mostly in the hands of elderly fishermen. Both photographs below opposite, were taken in August 1938 of the 3 ton zulu-type line fishing yawl *Willing Boys* BCK 251 at Portknockie, Banffshire.

Both these views show sailing traders of Dundee. The one above is rather interesting because the Norwegian ketch behind the stern of the *Mary* of Arbroath has a pole mast directly in front of the main mast. On this is a yard for setting a square sail.

Although not very distinct, the view of St Andrews above is one of the earliest photographs taken and shows sailing vessels in the early 1840s. It was taken within only a year or two of photography being discovered. The trading smack on the left has a yard on her mast and obviously used a square sail as part of her normal sail plan. Below is St Andrews some sixty years later. The topsail schooner here has four yards on the foremast and must have carried a considerable press of canvas.

Above we see Anstruther in 1910 crammed with fifies. These fishing luggers seem to almost fill the harbour. Numerically Anstruther was at its peak in about 1881 when it had 221 boats. The Scottish Fisheries Museum is at the other end of the Anstruther Harbour, just on the left of this photograph.

Opposite top is the *Jane & Maggies* KY 678 a typical east coast fifie. Some idea of the size of these powerful two masted luggers can be gathered from her dimensions. The keel length was 68 ft, beam 20 ft 9 in, depth 8 ft 2 in and the gross tonnage was 54.4. The *Jane & Maggies* was built in 1903 at the Anstruther yard of James N. Miller & Sons of St Monance. She was owned by Robert Ritchie who lived in Cellardyke but in 1912 this fifie was sold to Methil.

The *Jane & Maggies* was engaged in drift net and line fishing, but the small open boat seen below opposite at Crail, Fife, in 1913 is unloading lobster pots. The man in the boat is wearing leather boots.

The Scottish fishing craft whether from the east or west coast had the same characteristics. They all tended to be rather compact craft with little overhang at either ends and no rigging projecting. This was so that they could be packed tightly into small harbours. Also masts were placed as far forward and as far aft as possible leaving a large working space amidships. Although the zulus and fifies were magnificent craft, handling their gigantic lug sails at sea was dangerous. However, they may have clung so persistently to the lug sail because it was the only western European rig which could be set on a mast almost in the bows of a craft.

Prior to World War I there was a tremendous volume of trade in coal from the Firth of Forth across to nothern Europe. Above, there are eleven traders in Dysart Harbour and all bar one appear to be Scandinavian or Dutch. The Baltic vessels brought pit props and took coal back while the Dutch came to the Forth for either coal or stone for their sea defences. The tiny harbour which was then at West Wemyss saw the same trade. Opposite top is a topsail schooner at Kirkcaldy in 1904.

Opposite bottom is Bo'ness in about 1908. The paddle tugs are *Conquest*, *Lord Elgin* and *Venus*. This port has now silted up but for many years vast quantities of pitwood was imported here. A little further up the Forth was Grangemouth which had acres of timber basins full of Baltic timber. Much of this went to Glasgow saw-mills by canal barges. The Clyde timber trade was with Canada and for much of the nineteenth century about eighty square riggers left Greenock anchorage every spring for the St Lawrence, making two voyages a year. In the 1890s Alloa Dock, at the head of the Forth was full of Baltic timber ships with often a dozen or more waiting out in the channel for berths. Alloa declined after World War I but Scandinavian sailing ships and Orcadian ketches came to the Forth until World War II.

Charlestown-on-Forth seems to have typified a Victorian port. The harbour was not a natural one but was created in about 1765 by Charles, fifth Earl of Elgin, as an outlet for the mines and quarries on his estate.

Before a later Earl of Elgin sold out to a local company in 1860 the enterprise had reached such a scale that there was a railway carrying coal from the estate to Charlestown. The port must have been at its peak in 1880 when 200,000 tons of coal was shipped out. However, several of the Forth ports were having trouble with silting at about this time and the construction of wet docks began. Charlestown remained tidal and consequently slowly lost trade. This slow, almost casual, speed of operations suited the sailing ships and it remained a regular calling-place for the North Sea traders.

On the top of the opposite page is the Outer Harbour, Charlestown. The ships waiting to load are mostly Scandinavian. At the East Pier stern-on is the barquentine *Jordan* of Marstal which like so many Danish traders has her boat in the stern davits. Inside *Jordan* is the brig *Dannebrog*. Above is the Inner Harbour of Charlestown with the brig *Anna* drying her sails, and on the left, astern of the tug *Boreas*, is the *Neptunas* of Marstal under the chute waiting to load coal. Since the *Neptunas* is a schooner with four yards crossing her foremast, her correct definition is a standing topgallant yard schooner.

On the far left-hand side is the wooden barque *Meggie Dixon* of Amble at Capernaum Pier on 29 May 1884. Two men are on a stage recalking some seams below the waterline. The calking between planks was constantly working loose in wooden sailing ships. It was accepted that they all made a little water, but recalking was undertaken when pumping became excessive.

On the right of *Meggie Dixon* is a Baltic brigantine in the Inner Harbour, Leith, in about 1900. Below a topsail schooner is laid up in Inverkeithing. Below the waterline she has been sheathed with copper to protect her against boring worm in tropical waters.

Above on this page is the spratter *Blessing*, AA 38 at Alloa Dock in 1932. In the first decades of this century there were quite a number of spratters using stow-nets in both the Forth and Tay. In the winter of 1918 there were still at least twenty boats after sprat in the Tay. A few spratters from Kincardine on Forth worked in the season between Culross and Alloa while the *Blessing* was one of about a dozen working from Alloa.

Above are the Leith registered luggers at Port Seton on the south side of the Firth of Forth. These straight stem and stern boats were usually called fifies a little further north, but here they tended to be a little smaller and were sometimes called baldies. Below are the black sailed herring boats at Eyemouth in about 1910.

Adventure Sail

Although the working conditions on the old sailing ships were harsh, there were many people who got satisfaction from life aboard them and bitterly regretted their rapid departure from the seas. Sail held its own quite well until World War I, after that, although sail remained in a few specialised trades, generally speaking the western economics had no further use for wind-driven ships. Many devotees of sail collected information about them and the literature on them helped to keep alive the spirit of the fast-departing era. But despite the fact that the slow unpredictable sailing ships had no place in the new technological age, many people argued that a voyage in a sailing ship was a worthwhile experience.

The early advocates of sail training still thought in the old merchant navy terms of training under sail. They would like to have seen barques making ocean voyages which took many months and included at least one rounding of Cape Horn. A lot of young men would have jumped at the chance, but in the depressed conditions of the inter-war years such a scheme was unrealistic. At least people

thought so in Britain, but other European countries did build new square riggers for training under sail. Nazi Germany particularly saw it as a way of producing 'healthy youth' and embarked on an ambitious building programme While Norway even now gives all merchant officers a spell under sail and has the lowest accident rate in the world

Gradually a new approach was adopted, taking away the brutal conditions of the old days and making sail training an adventure, not an ordeal. In the late 1930s the Outward Bound School brought this ideal to reality with the schooner *Prince Louis*. In 1951 she was given to the Moray Sea School and while operated by them we see her above leaving Aberdeen. This 78 ft German ex-pilot schooner had been built at Bremerhaven in 1878.

Above is the schooner *Prince Louis* at sea while below she is entering Burghead a small harbour on the Moray Firth. The schooner's permanent crew consisted of a master, bo'sun, engineer and cook and on each cruise twenty young people could be carried. In the 1950s the value of sail training for those who did not intend making a career at sea was only just beginning to be widely accepted in the Western World.

The *Prince Louis* was replaced in 1955 by a three masted Baltic trading schooner which was renamed *Prince Louis II*. This schooner had only been built in 1944 and remained with the school until 1967. Above is a foredeck scene on *Prince Louis II*, on the right can be seen the bowline holding the forestaysail. This schooner could carry twenty-four young men as well as the regular crew. Right, we see her at sea.

When sail training started, yachts and work boats were bought and lent to give young people a chance to get to sea under sail. The ideal, perhaps due to the publicity the Tall Ships Race received, gained public sympathy and people and organisations eventually gave money for the building of new ships. It is a strange fact that people will contribute quite generously to the cost of a new vessel, but it is very much more difficult to raise money for the annual maintenance.

The sail trainers are doubly expensive to run because they are both sailing ships and fully powered motor vessels. Most of the sail trainers have been given rigs which were based on those evolved in the late nineteenth century. However, their underwater lines are based on those of a modern ocean racer. Opposite below can be seen the shapely hull of the STA schooner *Malcolm Miller* about to be launched at John Lewis & Sons, Aberdeen on 8 October 1967.

Above, the same schooner is seen shortly after leaving Leith on 10 March, 1968 at the start of her maiden voyage. Having a deckhouse but no cargo hatches, the designers could give the schooner a bridge between the main and mizzen masts. From here there is a better vision than the trading schooners had with their wheels right aft.

Above left is the 60 gross ton motor schooner *Robert Gordon*, built in the Netherlands in 1968 and run by the Robert Gordon School of Navigation, Aberdeen. On the right is the former West Country trading ketch *Isabel* at Troon. Under Captain Neil McKie, she sails on some training cruises from Loch Ryan.

Above is the three masted standing topgallant yard training schooner *Captain Scott*. The schooner's master, Commander Victor Clark says that in this view the square sails are not quite braced correctly so that they are not giving their full drawing power. The interesting point about this 144 ft-long Plockton-based schooner is that she has a wooden hull. The fishing industry has kept alive wooden shipbuilding on the Scottish East Coast while it has faded away in most other areas. The *Captain Scott* was built by Herd & Mackenzie, Buckie and launched on 7 September, 1971 for the Loch Eil Trust. Although she has all contemporary fittings, from the distance she looks like a magnificent ghost from the past.

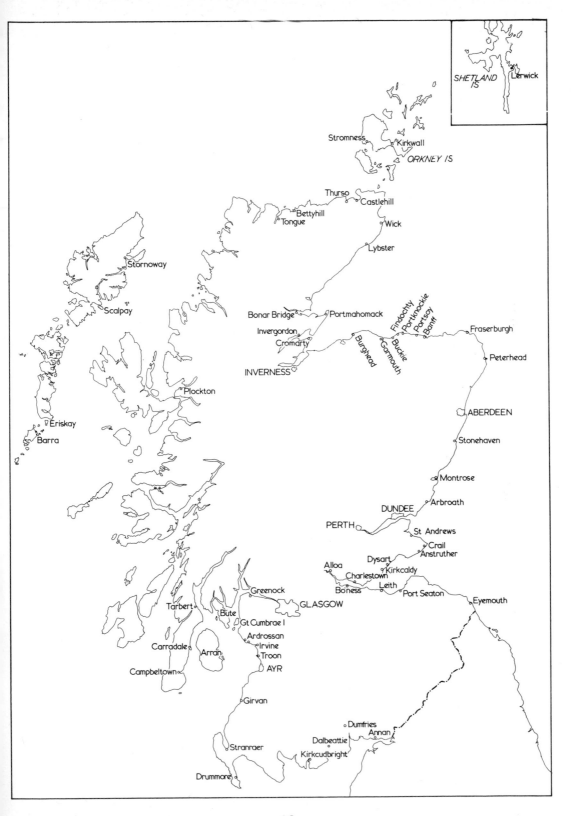

SHETLAND IS
Lerwick

Stromness
Kirkwall
ORKNEY IS

Thurso
Castlehill
Bettyhill
Tongue
Wick
Lybster

Stornoway

Scalpay

Bonar Bridge
Portmahomack
Invergordon
Cromarty
Burghead
Findochty
Portknockie
Portsoy
Banff
Fraserburgh
Buckie
Garmouth
Peterhead
INVERNESS

Plockton

Eriskay
Barra

ABERDEEN

Stonehaven

Montrose
Arbroath
DUNDEE
PERTH
St Andrews
Crail
Anstruther
Dysart
Alloa
Kirkcaldy
Charlestown
Boness
Leith
Greenock
Port Seaton
Eyemouth
Tarbert
GLASGOW
Bute
Gt Cumbrae I
Ardrossan
Carradale
Irvine
Arran
Troon
AYR
Campbeltown

Girvan

Dumfries
Annan
Stranraer
Dalbeattie
Kirkcudbright
Drummore

One of the pleasant parts about writing a book on a subject you are deeply interested in is that it puts you in contact with those of similar interests. The World Ship Society were able to tell me which of their members were keen on sail. With the Clyde square riggers, like the ships themselves the interest was international. Help came from the energetic Mills B. Lane Jr of Savannah and from Gustav Alexandersson of Sweden who allowed me to draw from his research. No serious book on sail in this period could be completed without reference to *Sea Breezes* over the years. Also *The Beaver* has been helpful.

Michael Bouquet who has written two books in this series has pointed me in the right direction of research on numerous occasions and Trevor Vincett gave me some practical advice on schooner sailing. Charles and Janet Harker's timely move to Dumfries allowed them to be helpful with this book as well as its predecessor *East Coast Sail*. Charles on one occasion actually sailed from Kirkcudbright in the smack *Iris*, which has no engine, to Arran and back just to collect an illustration. They were also able to introduce me to Mr James Kingan who during his extensive business career had been a Solway schooner owner.

Miss May Harvey of Maidens sent me some interesting family stories and James B. Thomson of Troon was able to supply me with information on his family's Solway traders and the west coast generally. Particularly helpful here were men with a lifetime spent on the coast, namely Walter Kerr of Millport, Duncan McCorquodale of Troon and also John MacFadyen of Oban. On the Clyde and particularly of the gabbarts Dan McDonald came to the rescue and was able to supply knowledge accumulated in many decades of intelligent study.

In the north of Scotland Peter Burr of Janetstown seems to be one of the few people to actively save material relating to local sailing coasters. As in so many cases his interest was actively sparked off by seeing the last sailers just before they vanished for ever. The Orkney Natural History Society have kindly allowed me to use a photograph from their book *Stromness, Late 19th Century Photographs*. My thanks to James G. Copland who went to sea in Shetland schooners before World War I and has many memories from the past, and thanks must go too to Peter Jamieson of Shetland. Around the Moray Firth R. Murray of Invergordon delved back into his memories and recalled the traders he knew and sailed on. Equally informative was James Slater, author of *Portsoy, Past and Present* and William S. Cumming of Buckie. There are many more people who each contributed facts about the past which have helped to build up this history. Their names would literally cover this page but to each one I extend grateful thanks.

On the fishing industry the Scottish Fisheries Museum, Anstruther, through its curator, G. T. Clarkson has done everything possible to assist in this photographic record. Mr G. A. Osbon was able to guide me through the National Maritime Museum's massive collection. Thanks again to G. F. Cordy who did most of the photographic work, and of course to my wife for her countless hours of typing.

Sources of Illustrations

The figures refer to the page numbers; the letters a or b indicate whether the picture is at the top or bottom of the page.

Aberdeen Journals 14, 87, 90a; Russ Lownds 15; Savannah Ships of the Sea Museum 16, 17a, b, 18, 19, 28; J. B. Thomson 20, 21, 38, 43b, 90b; J. Copland 22; James Kingan 23a; Graham Hussey 23b; Stewartry Museum, Kirkcudbright 24a; Miss S. Wood 24b; Wigtown County Library 7, 25, 26, 27a, b; Michael Bouquet 34, 50; Dan McDonald 13, 30a, b, 32b, 33, 38a, 44b, 46a, b, 47, 54b, 72b, 73b, 75b, c, 80b, 85; National Maritime Museum 31, 39, 40, 43a, 45, 78b; The Scottish Fisheries Museum 32a, 57, 69, 70, 71a, b, 72a, 73a, 74, 75a, 77b, 78a, 79, 80a, 84b, 86a, b; Miss Agnes Stewart 35; Walter Kerr 36, 37a; W. Belt 37b, 41, 44a, 66; John MacFadyen 48; John MacCorquodale 49; Peter Burr 51a, b, 52, 53a, b, 55a; Mrs C. W. Mackay 54, 54a; Stromness Museum 56; Peter Jamieson 58; B. J. R. Jamieson 59; John Mitchell 60; R. Murray 61; J. Machean 62, 63a, b; W. W. Cumming 65; A. W. Currie 67a, b; Mrs W. MacMillan 38b; P. A. Vicary 55b; Corporation of Dundee 76a b; The National Portrait Gallery 77a; Kirkcaldy Art Gallery and Museum 81; H. J. MacKenzie 1, 82, 83, 84a, c; Studio Tyrell 88a, b, 89b; G. F. Findlay 89a; Mrs D. Bromley-Martin 91a; John Dewar Studios 91b; Roger M. Smith 92; James Slater 64; Author 9, 29.

Index